THE
MIRACULOUS
JOURNEY

MARTY A. BULLIS

Regal

From Gospel Light
Ventura, California, U.S.A.

Published by Regal Books
From Gospel Light
Ventura, California, U.S.A.

Library of Congress Cataloging-in-Publication Data
Bullis, Marty A.
  The miraculous journey : anticipating God in the Christmas season / Marty A. Bullis.
    p. cm.
  ISBN 0-8307-4278-6 (hard cover)
  1. Advent—Prayers and devotions. 2. Christmas—Prayers and devotions. 3. Bible. N.T.
Gospels—Meditations. I. Title.
  BV40.B765 2006
  242'.33—dc22   2006021375

1   2   3   4   5   6   7   8   9   10   /   10   09   08   07

Rights for publishing this book in other languages are contracted by Gospel Light
Worldwide, the international nonprofit ministry of Gospel Light. For additional infor-
mation, visit www.gospellightworldwide.org.

DEDICATION

For Ann and George Pace,
who love the miracle of Jesus

CONTENTS

God. Is there any word in our language that is more central, critical, demanding? It looms majestically on the horizon, so emphatically and indisputably *there*. The word sends out tentacles, probing, looking for a way into our imaginations. David, in his magnificent God-poem, Psalm 18, opens with a cascade of God metaphors, seven of them:

Strength
Rock
Fortress
Deliverer
Shield
Horn of Salvation
Stronghold

7

But not just there in the way a mountain is there, an objective piece of geography that can be analyzed, mapped, climbed and photographed. The first-person personal pronoun, "my," is attached to each word. Everything we know of God is a matter of personal relationship. Nothing of God is simply a fact, a truth or an idea. And to make sure that we get it and never forget it, the verb that launches the sentence is *"I love"*—the most personal verb that we have in our lexicon.

And yet. And yet. And yet. Is there any word in our language that is more relentlessly marginalized, dismissed, depersonalized and blasphemed? What's going on here? How can a word—a *Person!*—so present to us, so centering to our lives, so dominant in every known language that men and women speak, be so easily and frequently reduced to a tired cliché?

It turns out that as comprehensive and welcoming, as personal and available as God is, when it comes right down to it, we would rather be our own gods. The all-time favorite strategy for accomplishing this is to change all the God-words into me-words. It is much less intellectually strenuous and emotionally taxing than denying God outright. It's a simple matter of grammatical sleight of hand: Rearrange a few words, and there it is. The devil was right: "Ye shall be as gods."

Those of us who take up membership in the Christian community have our work cut out for us. The Church has never spent a lot of its time trying to convince people that God exists. But it has had its hands full in convincing us that we are not gods. One of the Church's strategies has been the observance of Advent.

Advent opens the Church year. Advent gets our attention. It interrupts a lot of our god-talk, most of which has nothing to do with God but everything to do with us, and immerses us in stories of God-in-action—God comes, God comes to us: "Our God comes, he does not keep silence" (Ps. 50:3). "Advent" means "comes to"—*God* comes to *us*. God comes to us in the prophets; God comes to us in Jesus; God comes to us in acts of worship and giving and receiving in Jesus' name. Get used to it!

Advent is not an argument that God exists. It is an immersion in song and story and celebration that God *comes*—to us! It counters our pervasive assumptions that we are our own gods and supplants them with the glorious Advent of God in our history, in our lives. Listen to these stories; sing these songs; celebrate these comings and goings of God in this land. Did anyone tell a story of the god *you* like this? Did anyone ever compose and sing a song of the god *you* like this?

Welcome Marty Bullis as a companion for this Advent. Let him embrace you in prayer and meditation and reflection through these four Advent weeks. He is so good at this, purging our imaginations of our god-pretensions and clearing out time and space for celebration of God as He comes to us in Jesus.

Eugene H. Peterson
Professor Emeritus of Spiritual Theology
Regent College, Vancouver, B.C.

ACKNOWLEDGMENTS

In late fall 2003 I pulled together a community of friends with whom I wanted to remember and celebrate Jesus' Advent. Our goals were to read afresh the Gospel stories of Jesus' birth, to pray, and to journal daily. My task was to write devotions to accompany our observance. Weekly (sometimes daily) I would e-mail or print reflections for the group, and on Sunday those who lived nearby gathered to talk and pray. It was a wonderful Advent season, the fruit of which comes to you inside this book. That first group included Don and Jill Blake, Tracie Bullis, Jeff and Mary Beth Eyet, George and Ann Pace, and Karen Wood—without their encouragement this book wouldn't have been written

In 2004 the text found its way to churches across the United States. The following people were instrumental in making this happen: Danny and Lisha White, Bill and Madeline Bullis, Tom Hay, Tom Oster, Lee Morrison, Pat Bruce, Bill and Carol Moore, Anne Ross, Deborah Dail, Merry Meloy, Skip Hastings, Laurel Dolan, Donna and Bill White, Dan and Lori Speak, Esther Smith, Kathryn Johnson, Steve Cort, Lois Jackson, Eugene and Jan Peterson, Roger Rath, Terry and Elena Stewart, Marguerite Shuster, and Mabel Finch.

I wish to thank the following congregations who generously supported this book in 2004: First Presbyterian Church—Philipsburg, PA; Denbigh Presbyterian Church—Chesapeake, VA;

Elkton Presbyterian Church—Elkton, VA; First Baptist Church—Fountain Valley, CA; Christ Lutheran Church—Whitefish, MT; Knox Presbyterian Church—Pasadena, CA; First Presbyterian Church and Trinity United Methodist—Philipsburg, PA; Kylertown Presbyterian Church—Kylertown, PA; First Presbyterian Church—Harrisonburg, VA; Christ Church—Oak Brook, IL; Chapel by the Lake—Juneau, AK; La Verne Heights Presbyterian Church—La Verne, CA; and, Christ Our King Presbyterian Church—Bel Air, MD.

Finally, my thanks to you, the reader, for celebrating Jesus' Advent with saints all around the world.

Christmas is coming . . . a season of arrivals! Friends will come to our homes; grown children will return to their parents to celebrate and feast. Physical objects will get caught up with us in the movement—trees will be tied in place with fishing line, stockings will be hung and presents will start appearing. Anticipation keeps us on our toes as we get moving.

These events are good fuel for reflection, good opportunities to revisit the story of Christ's Advent. Christ entered the world in motion: traveling to visit Elizabeth while in Mary's womb, journeying to Bethlehem to be born, visiting Jerusalem with His parents weeks after His stable birth, and fleeing to Egypt to avoid King Herod's wrath. His early days and months were as harried as any modern life could offer. Yet this child, this Word-made-flesh, brought stability into a tumultuous world. The Gospel accounts of His Advent give us a close-up look at Christ and can help us prepare again for His arrival in this Christmas season. As we immerse ourselves in these stories, we can ready our hearts to hear again the good news: "Peace to all men and women on earth who please him" (Luke 2:14, *THE MESSAGE*).

One of my mentors, a 94-year-old Benedictine priest, shared a story with me one afternoon. He said he'd recently eaten an oyster that had been delivered to his plate from half a world away. As he cracked open the shell, he paused. He was struck by the thought that the oyster had traveled league upon league and not been affected by anything until his knife had completed its work. The priest was reminded of his own journeys around the globe in service to his monastic order. He'd traveled far and wide and not been cracked open by the world's knife. He finished his story and looked at me with his wizened Belgian eyes. Then he lifted his index finger slightly and said, "Do not confuse stability with immobility. One can be stable while in motion." As we gear up for motion this holiday season, as we prepare for all the arrivals, stability awaits us in the life of Christ—stability in motion.

———

What follows are daily Scripture readings for the Advent season accompanied by short reflections, bidding prayers, and space for journaling.

Start by reading the Scripture passage for the day. (Due to space considerations, longer Gospel readings are not printed in their entirety. An asterisk [*] following "The Gospel Reading" indicates where the excerpt provides the day's full Scripture reading. On other days, have your Bible handy so that you can read the entire passage found in the citation.)

Pause and meditate on the parts of the Scripture that strike you. Next, read the accompanying reflection that focuses on an aspect of the Gospel passage. Following the reflection, set aside a few minutes for prayer as you open your heart to God. A four-part bidding prayer is provided to guide you. Rest in silence for a short time at the end of each prayer. The final prayer asks God to enliven your spirit as you write your thoughts to Him during the time of journaling. This fourfold structure (Scripture, reflection, prayer, journaling) moves us from hearing God's Word to receiving this word in our spirit and then responding to this word in prayer and deed.

There are 29 devotions—7 for each week of Advent, plus 1 for Christmas Day. The devotions begin in Matthew's Gospel and work their way through Mark's, Luke's and John's accounts. Devotions for Sundays will take slightly longer because they involve reading the entire Advent story from the week's Gospel. The other six days of each week focus on brief sections of the week's Gospel. No journaling space is provided on Sundays, in observation of the Sabbath day of rest.

Depending upon the calendar year, Christmas can fall as early as the Monday of week four or as late as the Sunday following week four. I have included a full week's devotions for week four. If Christmas falls early in the week, you may choose to continue the devotions throughout the week or jump ahead and use the devotion entitled "Christmas Day."

The devotional is well suited for use by small groups that meet during Advent. An "Advent Litany for Small Groups" is included as a guide for structuring group meetings. The litany includes responsive readings and time for discussion and silent reflection. Advent candle-lighting meditations for Church and home are also included at the end of the book. May God's peace and stability be yours as you relive Jesus' miraculous journey!

———

The Word became flesh and dwelt among us, full of grace and truth; we have beheld his glory, glory as of the only Son from the Father.

John 1:14, *RSV*

PART ONE

THE FIRST WEEK OF ADVENT

SEVEN DEVOTIONS FROM MATTHEW

The birth of Jesus took place like this . . .
Matthew 1:18, *THE MESSAGE*

THE GOSPEL READING
Matthew 1–2, *THE MESSAGE*

THE REFLECTION
A BLOODY BEGINNING

Jesus' entrance into the world was not peaceful, though the American Christmas industry—replete with smiling nativity animals and happy holy-family Christmas cards—would have us believe so. From the beginning, Christ's presence was a disruption of the everyday and a wresting of peaceful human emotions. His entrance into our world was a confrontation, with no room given for avoiding this person, not even while still a fetus. Joseph had to face the fact that the child in Mary's womb was not his heir. Only a visitation by an angel of the Lord kept him from divorce. Wise men were moved to rise up from their places in the East, to undertake a long journey and to pay Him homage. This child even disrupted the political scene. He was viewed as a threat to the king while just a toddler. Not even two years old, He was enough of a threat to power that Herod massacred an entire population of boys to rid himself

people whose contributions are important to name. A bit of sleuthing reveals that this chain of people who contributed to the birth of Christ was far from perfect. We find all sorts of lives: kings, a prostitute, refugees, adulterers, people who were faithful, crooked, peaceful, jealous, righteous, twisted and humble.

Looking at Christ's family wall—the bricks of ancestors—is an exercise in hope. His family is normal, not chock-full of exalted characters, perhaps even containing more than its share of troubled relatives. Yet this history, the acts of these people, does not dictate who Christ will be. His life is a blending of the divine and the human. A perfect divinity melded to mucky humanity. Eternality redeeming a corrupted ancestry. We see in Christ that God has formed a person who is able to redeem family history. Not only did He redeem that of His earthly father, but He also redeemed that of all human families. Christ's work is to redeem people and make right the lines of descent. As we look forward to celebrating the birth of Jesus, we are assured that as we look back—into His history and our own—these rows of bricks are not the end of the story. Redemption awaits humanity, and its advent is the incarnation—the enfleshing—of Christ.

THE BIDDING PRAYER

Come, Lord Jesus! (silence)
Ready my spirit to receive You this day. (silence)
Show me how You are at work that I might serve You better. (silence)
Enliven my spirit as I reveal myself to You in written word. (silence)

THE JOURNAL

*Her husband Joseph, being a righteous man and unwilling to
expose her to public disgrace, planned to dismiss her quietly.
But just when he had resolved to do this, an angel of the Lord
appeared to him in a dream and said . . .*

Matthew 1:19-20, *NRSV*

THE GOSPEL READING
Matthew 1:18-25, *NRSV*

THE REFLECTION
A HOLY DREAM

Dreams while we're asleep are strange things. Some people build
their lives around them, trying to understand their importance to
waking life. Some people, who fancy themselves more rational, scoff
at all the ballyhoo attached to interpreting the unconscious, thinking it too irrational to merit consideration. Like Ebenezer Scrooge,
they chalk up disturbing images to undigested bits of dinner or to
chemical imbalances. Americans by and large have bought into the
idea that sleep-thoughts are marginal. We may recount a vivid
dream to a friend or spouse, but seldom does the conversation go
farther than the response, "Hmmm, that *is* weird!" Once in a while a
dream captures us; it hits home and becomes the symbol for our life

situation. These God-inspired thoughts grip us far more completely than any rational waking exercise we pursue. Perhaps this is why God chose to speak to Joseph through an angel, in a dream.

Joseph's problem, one that undoubtedly consumed his waking life, was that he was engaged to a woman who had mothered a child without his assistance. We imagine that Mary told Joseph the entire story of the angel's visitation to her—it's hard to imagine that she could have remained silent about this to him. But what rational man, what man awake from the shoulders up, could believe such a story? Probably there is none.

Then comes God's voice, in the person of an angel, to an un-awake man. To a man in a most helpless state. To a man "caught" sleeping. Is there irony here? "Do I have your attention, Joseph? This child is mine. And I need you to care for Him. He needs a name, and you will name Him, 'Jesus.'" Even though we walk away from God's voice in our rational world, He has ways of helping us pay attention. Perhaps instead of slapping one another in the face with the words "Wake up!" we need to say, "Sleep! And listen!"

THE BIDDING PRAYER

Come, Lord Jesus! (silence)
Ready my spirit to receive You this day. (silence)
Show me how You are at work that I might serve You better. (silence)
Enliven my spirit as I reveal myself to You in written word. (silence)

THE JOURNAL

Wise men from the East came to Jerusalem, asking, "Where is the child who has been born king of the Jews? For we observed his star at its rising, and have come to pay him homage." When King Herod heard this, he was frightened, and all Jerusalem with him . . .

Matthew 2:1-3, *NRSV*

THE GOSPEL READING
Matthew 2:1-6, *NRSV*

THE REFLECTION
A HOLY COMING

Thanksgiving and Christmas are times of comings. We start Advent with Thanksgiving comings fresh in our mind and with anticipation of Christmas comings that are not far off. We look forward to visits from family and friends. There is delight in fixing meals and decorating our homes, offering ourselves, and hoping that people will enjoy what we have done with our hands. At times during this rush of seasons, some of us get neurotic about the preparations. We need attention paid to our works. We want recognition for what we've been about. The line between delight and neurosis is sometimes a thin one for us broken humans.

In the person of Christ, we have a human who will never cross this line. He comes into the world having accomplished nothing, yet He is worshiped. He exits the world having brought salvation, yet He is scorned. He walks the entire way, from incarnation to crucifixion, needing no affirmation. He is content to simply be and do what He is.

In the person of Herod, we see humanity at its worst, placed in relief opposite the Christ child. We have a king whose subjects are so dependent upon his emotional whims that when he is troubled they all must be troubled with him. Like a moody spouse who wants to be coaxed out of his Christmas decorating fit, we see this king presiding over a city of people as if he were a sponge soaking up all of their energy. For one like this, there can be no worship, no falling down before another in awe, but only self-centered leeching.

Christ will have none of this. He chose from eternity to enter the world through a broken family, in a city regarded as insignificant, and in the form of a helpless child. Yet in this we see the ways of God, where the least are greatest, where the poor are rich, where the meek inherit the earth. This Christ child is a King who can *lead* His people, not merely lord them, and who does not force them to mirror His emotional state. He is a babe who does not require our worship but evokes it as only an *un*-needy God can.

THE BIDDING PRAYER

Come, Lord Jesus! (silence)
Ready my spirit to receive You this day. (silence)
Show me how You are at work that I might serve You better. (silence)
Enliven my spirit as I reveal myself to You in written word. (silence)

THE JOURNAL

Herod secretly called for the wise men and learned from them the exact time when the star had appeared. Then he sent them to Bethlehem . . .

. . . having been warned in a dream not to return to Herod, they left for their own country by another road.

Matthew 2:7-8,12 *NRSV*

THE GOSPEL READING
Matthew 2:7-12 *NRSV*

30

THE REFLECTION
WORSHIPING THE KING

The wise men came to Jerusalem and asked around, "Where is the child that will be king?" This was a dangerous question for men who did not know the disposition of the king. Had Herod been a good king, a secure king, the question would have been appropriate. But this was a king full of himself and his power. He was a king full of the insecurities that come with fears of losing power. The wise men's question evoked fear in the king and a resulting wave of fear in the people—his was fear of losing power and theirs was fear of losing their lives as the king became emotionally unstable.

Though fearful and insecure, Herod could not simply act out. He needed these wise men to show him the boy who would be king. So he entered into a game of power with them—a game that insecure men of power know well. The first move was to call them to his chamber in secret. He knew the troubles that a public meeting would produce—what would happen if the populace heard that the king wanted to know about this new ruler-to-be. The next move was a lie. He said that he desired to worship the boy. It was a dark act that reflected the black depths of a human soul gone awry.

We see in the wise men's audience with the infant Christ a different picture of the human soul. It is the image of a soul in submission, a picture of humility. Matthew tells us that these men fell to their knees and worshiped. Worship is an act of giving up one's control, of surrendering one's life to another. It is an act we rarely do well because we rarely let go of our self and its interests for long. But here we see, in this act of kneeling, the manifestation of souls surrendered. Their pilgrimage, their lavish gifts and the prostration of their bodies show the great heights a human soul attains when it has found that one thing worthy of losing itself to.

THE BIDDING PRAYER

Come, Lord Jesus! (silence)
Ready my spirit to receive You this day. (silence)
Show me how You are at work that I might serve You better. (silence)
Enliven my spirit as I reveal myself to You in written word. (silence)

THE JOURNAL

*Now after they had left, an angel of the Lord appeared
to Joseph in a dream and said . . .*

Matthew 2:13, *NRSV*

THE GOSPEL READING
Matthew 2:13-15, *NRSV*

THE REFLECTION
THE SECOND DREAM—FLEE EVIL

34

It is difficult to leave one's place in the world, but when children we love are in danger, nothing will move us faster. The flight into Egypt has been the subject of countless works of art because it is a central theme for human beings: protection of a family in the face of evil. We are given no hint that Joseph's and Mary's lives were endangered by the news the wise men shared with Herod. The slaughter to which Matthew alludes in these verses, and which is soon accomplished, does not extend to the parents of the children. But this does not matter. A loving mother and father would rather give up their lives than see such evil overtake their child.

This second dream of Joseph's gets our attention. God is speaking. And this method of dream-messaging is familiar to us now. The message comprises a series of commands: *get up, take, flee, remain.* The staccato rhythm of these imperatives gets our attention. They require action in the face of evil. The Lord is telling Joseph just what he needs to hear. The words and their arrangement have their intended impact: Joseph gets up, takes his family, flees by night and remains in Egypt.

We are called to care for those around us, as Joseph cared for his family. Evil is abundant in this life, but far more plentiful is the voice of God. We can depend upon this voice as Joseph, in a very short time, had come to depend upon it. It is a voice that is razor sharp when it needs to be, yet passionate about our welfare. Why? We are children of the speaker. Nothing will move God faster than caring for the welfare of His children in the face of evil.

THE BIDDING PRAYER

Come, Lord Jesus! (silence)
Ready my spirit to receive You this day. (silence)
Show me how You are at work that I might serve You better. (silence)
Enliven my spirit as I reveal myself to You in written word. (silence)

THE JOURNAL

*When Herod saw that he had been tricked by the wise men, he was
infuriated, and he . . .*

Matthew 2:16, *NRSV*

THE GOSPEL READING
Matthew 2:16-23, *NRSV*

THE REFLECTION
A FURIOUS RAGE

38

Most of us have been in a furious rage at some point in our lives,
though none of us has ordered the slaughter of an entire city of boys
under the age of two. There is a rage that comes upon us when we do
not get our way, when our wishes are not followed or there is no
response to our commands. We want our way, and it doesn't really
matter why someone didn't get it (i.e., our way) done. We'll have them
for lunch if they don't watch out. It's easy for us to view Herod as evil
and ourselves as beyond such problems. But then again, we have
never controlled an entire country, never been used to everyone ful-
filling our slightest whim, never had an army that could implement
our wishes. We probably are not as far from Herod as we might think.

It is the evil in Herod and in us all that is the reason for Christ's
entrance into the world. The Scriptures tell us, "There is no one

who is righteous, not even one" (Romans 3:10, *NRSV*). This baby enters a world that wants to eat Him alive. But He doesn't respond to that evil intent. Christ responds to the needs of the world. We read in Philippians, "Christ Jesus, who, though he was in the form of God, did not regard equality with God as something to be [clung to at all costs], but emptied himself, taking the form of a slave, being born in human likeness. And being found in human form, he humbled himself and became obedient" (2:5-8, *NRSV*, brackets mine).

He chooses to come into the world as we all do—helpless. It is a moving picture. A King who chooses to be helpless set against a king who chooses to grasp power and destroy anything that would stand in his way. We are of the kin of those who would hold power. If we seem far from Herod's sin, it is only because Christ fights for us. His strength (as ours must be) is obedience and humility—an emptying of self.

THE BIDDING PRAYER

Come, Lord Jesus! (silence)
Ready my spirit to receive You this day. (silence)
Show me how You are at work that I might serve You better. (silence)
Enliven my spirit as I reveal myself to You in written word. (silence)

THE JOURNAL

PART TWO

THE SECOND WEEK OF ADVENT

SEVEN DEVOTIONS FROM MARK

The good news of Jesus Christ—the Message!—begins here,
following to the letter the scroll of the prophet Isaiah.

Watch closely: I'm sending my preacher ahead of you;
He'll make the road smooth for you. Thunder in the desert!
Prepare for God's arrival! Make the road smooth and straight!

Mark 1:1-3, *THE MESSAGE*

THE GOSPEL READING
Mark 1:1-15, *THE MESSAGE*

44

THE REFLECTION
A WAY PREPARED

Mark's is a different Advent account from Matthew's—it's not the story usually chosen for readings during the Christmas season. Unlike Matthew's and Luke's accounts, Mark bypasses Jesus' birth and childhood in order to get immediately to the Christ's adult work: bringing salvation to a dead world. There is a sense of urgency in Mark's writing that we find in none of the other Gospels—a sense that Christ is active and moving quickly in our world. Jesus is presented full of power and the Spirit of God.

John the baptizer tells us that the Christ who will come after him is "more powerful than I." As we'll see in Luke's Advent story

next week, John's parents, Elizabeth and Zechariah, had been promised by an angel of God that their child would have the power and
spirit of Elijah, one of Israel's most powerful prophets. Yet this
Christ will be stronger. What a different introduction to Jesus! We
are forced by this Advent story to leap forward past 30 of Jesus'
growing-up years, past the swaddling clothes and manger, forced to
see the incarnation as preparation for a future advent—the advent
of *Gospel* in a world emptied of good news.

We have the barest hint of the incarnation story as we listen to
God calling, "You are my Son, the Beloved." Our imagination
springs on the word "Son," and we wonder how a blood-relative of
God came to be in our world. The immediacy of the account leaves
us wanting to race forward through Christ's life; but the account
also makes our mind want to review history. When we read the
words "the time is fulfilled" for the coming of the Kingdom, we
want to run into the past. We are full of questions: How did the
time get fulfilled? Where was this Christ before He walked down to
the Jordan? Why wasn't it in the papers? Why didn't we hear about
it? We are caught between past and future, anticipation and imaginative memory. Mark's account leaves us surprised, leaves our
minds racing backward and forward.

THE BIDDING PRAYER

Come, Lord Jesus! (silence)
Ready my spirit to receive You this day. (silence)
Show me how You are at work that I might serve You better. (silence)
Enliven my spirit as I reveal myself to You in written word. (silence)

THE GOSPEL READING*

The beginning of the good news of Jesus Christ, the Son of God.
Mark 1:1, *NRSV*

THE REFLECTION
A NEW BEGINNING

Mark's theme at the start of his Gospel is *repentance*—getting us back on track, starting us anew. He captures us with his opening word: "beginning," *archê* in Greek. *Archê* is a central concept to Gospel, where time is renewed, lives started again. John's Gospel opens with the word: "In the beginning [*archê*]" (1:1, *NRSV*), and Luke uses it in the opening lines of his Gospel, speaking of "those who from the beginning [*archê*] were eyewitnesses and servants of the word" (1:2, *NRSV*). The word *archê* draws us in and produces a longing in us. We want to be in on *archê*—we don't want to miss a thing. Like the play we're dying to see, or the concert we've waited months to hear, we don't want to be caught in traffic, unable to be there when the curtain rises.

As we read Mark during this Advent week, we are given a remarkable and sacred gift. We, like the eyewitnesses in Luke's story, have gotten in on this *archê*. We have four weeks of getting ready.

Four weeks of beginning again. Four weeks of waiting in our seats in anticipation. Four weeks to breathe a relaxed sigh, "I haven't missed it. It's coming! I even have time to get popcorn! To enjoy this thing!"

And here is the *archê*-enfleshed Christ, drawing us along. He's the one who has never missed anything. He's waiting for us to journey with Him to His birth. Time stops, reverses on itself and ticks in Bethlehem again. Time whirrs past and leaps forward to the new beginning—the next advent of Christ—to the paradox where beginning and end become one. Christ, the Alpha and Omega, bookends our lives (and time itself) as we shout, "He's here! In God-time! We haven't missed anything."

THE BIDDING PRAYER

Come, Lord Jesus! (silence)
Ready my spirit to receive You this day. (silence)
Show me how You are at work that I might serve You better. (silence)
Enliven my spirit as I reveal myself to You in written word. (silence)

THE JOURNAL

THE GOSPEL READING*

As it is written in the prophet Isaiah, "See, I am sending my messenger ahead of you, who will prepare your way; the voice of one crying out in the wilderness: 'Prepare the way of the Lord, make his paths straight.'"
Mark 1:2-3, *NRSV*

THE REFLECTION
MAKING THINGS STRAIGHT

We're often crooked—we even like being crooked. I'm talking about our sins here. It's not easy to live a straight life. Ask anyone who's suffering from some type of addiction. And by the way, we're all addicts, so ask the next person you see. Crookedness is part of the human condition.

It wasn't meant to be like this and, luckily for us, crookedness is not part of God's condition. God loves walking straight roads; He loves to straighten our paths. This "way" that John the baptizer is sent ahead to straighten is *us*—you and me. It's not as if Christ comes into the world for a vacation or to take a relaxing cruise around the Mediterranean. He comes into the world to walk into us, to walk *through* our lives. We're His path, what He came to be about. You saw this coming, didn't you? Straightening Christ's path, preparing Christ's way, means getting us straightened out. For His goal is to live *in* us and make our souls a rich garden both for His and our own enjoyment.

John's message is important, for it is a message to us. It comprises two commands: Prepare the way and make straight the paths. The way is through humanity—the paths are you and me. But the amazing gift in this Advent, this announcement to get the road prepared, is that *we're* supposed to be doing this preparation. God enlists us to work for His kingdom. His walking ground is in our actions, in our lives, in our being. He wants to get rid of our boulders and rock slides, to clear dead branches from before His feet, to build bridges over our stagnant swamps, to blast away any impeding stiles.

This straightening is for our benefit as well as His. Crooked feels good when we do it, but it doesn't feel good afterward, and there is always the afterward. Plumb and square is the only thing that stands the test over the long haul. Ask any junkie if he likes being addicted and he'll tell you yes, when he's high. Crooked highs don't last. (Ask the next person through your door and surprise him or her with an Advent conversation.) Yet there is a high that comes through right living, from knowing that you are spending your energy preparing for the Lord. It's what we're made for. It's God's condition, and He intends it for us.

THE BIDDING PRAYER

Come, Lord Jesus! (silence)
Ready my spirit to receive You this day. (silence)
Show me how You are at work that I might serve You better. (silence)
Enliven my spirit as I reveal myself to You in written word. (silence)

THE JOURNAL

THE GOSPEL READING*

*John the baptizer appeared in the wilderness, proclaiming a baptism
of repentance for the forgiveness of sins. And people from the whole
Judean countryside and all the people of Jerusalem were going out to
him, and were baptized by him in the river Jordan, confessing their
sins. Now John was clothed with camel's hair, with a leather belt
around his waist, and he ate locusts and wild honey. He proclaimed,
"The one who is more powerful than I is coming after me; I am not
worthy to stoop down and untie the thong of his sandals. I have baptized
you with water; but he will baptize you with the Holy Spirit."*

Mark 1:4-8, *NRSV*

54

THE REFLECTION
ONE MORE WORTHY

It's not easy to keep the thought in mind that there is a person we're
not worthy to be around. Try focusing for any length of time on the
idea that there's someone whose Birkenstocks or Nikes you're not
graceful enough to buckle or lace up. We're so used to thinking of
ourselves as equals and giving ourselves self-esteem pep talks that,
more often than not, we think of ourselves as better than the rest
of the world. Consider two lines of thought: (1) "People would

pretty lucky to have me around! I'm a valuable asset to the community. Don't forget it!" (2) "Her shoe? Are you kidding? I'm not good enough to lay a little finger on it." Which line sounds more like the stuff of reality TV? Truth is, we feel very comfortable with our selves—even those of us with self-esteem problems.

But someone out there is more grace-full, more power-full, more worthy than we are. Next to him or her we look like slug bait. Not exactly the tingly Christmas-is-coming pick-me-up we've been looking for in Advent. We're in the same boat with John, even if we don't realize it. John—a star in God's kingdom work—couldn't hold a candle next to this Christ.

But notice what John tells the people (what he tells us) about this One-more-worthy. "He will baptize you with the Holy Spirit." This Advent—this "arrival" of the Christ—is a giving of Himself, of His Spirit, to those not worthy. It is as if the queen has stopped her carriage next to us to say, "*You* are my lost daughter. *You* are full of my spirit. Come and live with me." The arrival of Christ is our arrival into true personhood through the entrance of His Spirit into our very being.

The Bidding Prayer

Come, Lord Jesus! (silence)
Ready my spirit to receive You this day. (silence)
Show me how You are at work that I might serve You better. (silence)
Enliven my spirit as I reveal myself to You in written word. (silence)

THE JOURNAL

THE GOSPEL READING*

In those days Jesus came from Nazareth of Galilee and was baptized by John in the Jordan. And just as he was coming up out of the water, he saw the heavens torn apart and the Spirit descending like a dove on him. And a voice came from heaven, "You are my Son, the Beloved; with you I am well pleased."

Mark 1:9-11, *NRSV*

THE REFLECTION
BELOVED

Do you ever wonder about Joseph's first words to Jesus? Do you wonder how he greeted this young miracle? Joseph's holy dream provided him some time to contemplate the wonder of this child conceived by the Holy Spirit. Jesus, who was not Joseph's own flesh, who was not given to him as son, the child he is called to protect and for whom he becomes a legal guardian—what does he say to this child? We hope for a word of wonder. We hope Joseph was not resentful or unenthusiastic. We want a word of celebration for this baby—a smiling, leaping, light-the-cigars fatherly greeting. The relationship between Joseph and Jesus isn't given much play, however. The Gospels emphasize a different relationship, the relationship with another parent—the Father who hung the moon. This is the relationship we all long for no matter how good our earthly fathers were and are.

Mark gives us the first recorded words of the Father to the Son. It's a perfect greeting that includes an affirmation of family, an assurance of love and an encouraging word about the Son's work. The Father says, "You're a part of me, My Son. I love you and I'm happy with what you've become." God's love-words point us back to Christ's growing-up years. He couldn't have come to the Jordan, He couldn't have received such affirmation, without a fruitful past. He has become a man in the fullest sense of the word, and His Father is proud.

God throws Jesus an impromptu party, with a celebratory display (a ripped-open heaven), and a gift (the Spirit coming upon Him like a dove). We are not so far from God in our encounters with children as to be unable to understand this divine encounter. Our human celebrations of relationship are infused with divinity. Relationship *is* a thing of the divine world, and our affinity with this scene shows how much our relationships, at their best, are shaped by God being in us.

THE BIDDING PRAYER

Come, Lord Jesus! (silence)
Ready my spirit to receive You this day. (silence)
Show me how You are at work that I might serve You better. (silence)
Enliven my spirit as I reveal myself to You in written word. (silence)

THE JOURNAL

THE GOSPEL READING*

*And the Spirit immediately drove him out into the wilderness.
He was in the wilderness forty days, tempted by Satan; and he
was with the wild beasts; and the angels waited on him.*

Mark 1:12-13, *NRSV*

THE REFLECTION
A MUCKY WORLD

62

There is no flight into Egypt in Mark's Gospel, no rescue for the
holy child from evil beings. We are shown a mature Christ, readied
for battle, whose adult advent in the world initiates the time of
confrontation. It is a time for standing His ground, not a time for
flight. Equipped from birth, now set apart through baptism, Jesus
is driven to make war with evil. Mark tells us that the Spirit, which
has just descended upon Jesus, takes Him out into the wilderness
to meet God's foe. The Spirit acts forcefully, driving Him out,
expelling Him, like a soldier equipped for battle being thrown into
the middle of the fight. All of Jesus' life has led to this confrontation. Herod may have seemed a threat to the child, but now the
child-grown-to-full-strength must meet His real threat.

Christ has been at the center of this battle all along, even while He was making a nighttime escape to Egypt. Only now is time fulfilled and readied for His active working. Now is the time when His arrival assures God's victory. The incarnation story provides us with a taste of this scene that is to come. The Christ-child divides the world into sidelines: those fearing Him and those worshiping Him. We know something will come of this. Mark lets us view the advent of a battle unlike any other. He shows us God walking out alone to endure all of our temptations. No human can fight this battle, for we have all fallen to the enemy. Guileless beasts and untainted angels alone can be with this Christ as He fights. He has come, made His Advent, to reclaim us. He has arrived for His fallen comrades.

63

THE BIDDING PRAYER

Come, Lord Jesus! (silence)
Ready my spirit to receive You this day. (silence)
Show me how You are at work that I might serve You better. (silence)
Enliven my spirit as I reveal myself to You in written word. (silence)

THE JOURNAL

THE GOSPEL READING*

Now after John was arrested, Jesus came to Galilee, proclaiming the good news of God, and saying, "The time is fulfilled, and the kingdom of God has come near; repent, and believe in the good news."

Mark 1:14-15, *NRSV*

THE REFLECTION
REPENT AND BELIEVE

66

Belief was always the goal of Christ's Advent. We've seen some of the believers who circled around the Christ-child. We've seen an evil king who refused to believe. Sin keeps us from belief, causes a cessation of belief. It happens each day, little by little: We wander away from believing. We are weak; we have difficulty charting a straight path. Belief, though present, often wavers in us. We live much of our lives as if we are given over to a spouse who does not love us, as if we are trapped in an abusive marriage, drained of any energy for change. John Donne describes himself and us in his poem "Batter My Heart."

> I, like a usurped town, to another due,
> Labor to admit You, but oh to no end!
> Reason, Your viceroy in me, should defend,

But is captived, and proves weak or untrue.
Yet dearly I love You, and would be lovèd fain,
But am betrothed unto Your enemy:

Christ returns from His encounter with evil with a ready message on His lips: "Believe!" He understands that we're weak (He couldn't take us into the wilderness for fear we'd be lost), but He proclaims His message anyway. His command brings our ears to attention; we sit up, longing to hear who is preaching salvation to us. We want to get with the program again. We shout with Donne:

Divorce me, untie, or break that knot again,
Take me to You, imprison me, for I
Except You enthrall me, never shall I be free,
Nor ever chaste, except You ravish me.[2]

This Christ returns from the wilderness knowing that we remain weak; but He has a message of encouragement for us. "The kingdom of God has come near. And by the way, you should know that I can win this thing—I can win you back." We may be weak, but Christ now controls the battlefield.

Alone in the wilderness, alone at the cross, Christ fights a battle we cannot enter. He endures what we are unable to. His first sermon is given with the taste of victory in His mouth. We can taste it too when we chew on His proclamation: "Repent! Believe! I have broken the knot!"

THE BIDDING PRAYER

Come, Lord Jesus! (silence)
Ready my spirit to receive You this day. (silence)
Show me how You are at work that I might serve You better. (silence)
Enliven my spirit as I reveal myself to You in written word. (silence)

THE JOURNAL

Part Three

The Third Week of Advent

Seven Devotions from Luke

*Since I have investigated all the reports in close detail,
starting from the story's beginning, I decided to write it all out
for you, most honorable Theophilus, so you can know beyond the
shadow of a doubt the reliability of what you were taught.*
Luke 1:3-4, *THE MESSAGE*

THE GOSPEL READING
Luke 1:1–2:39, *THE MESSAGE*

THE REFLECTION
A FULL BIRTH STORY

Going from Mark's opening chapter into Luke's birth narrative is
like moving from a deli take-out meal to a rich seven course dinner. Luke is generous with details and desirous of providing an
orderly account of the Advent of our Lord. It's a bit daunting to
take in all of this in a single week of daily devotions. Where do we
start? There seems to be too much to chew on, too much to soak
up. We wonder, *Why didn't I spend all four weeks in Luke's story?*

Luke's is the type of story you would like to hear from your
mother 40 years after your birth. "Tell me how I was born, Mom."
We want someone who takes the time to give a biography of our
beginning, someone who doesn't want to rush or miss any of the
important details. Many of us don't have an account like this, don't
have mothers with great memories or family members doting on
our history. But in Luke we have something to whet our appetite for

birth history. God made sure we had a good account of how He brought His Son into the world. And though we may not have an account so rich recorded about us, God is as interested in our beginning and our story as He is in His own entrance into the world. For after all, God came walking into our lives as He entered the world. His Advent marks our own chance at rebirth; and rebirth encompasses the entire person: past, present and future.

We taste God's interest in humanity as we read John the baptizer's birth story. A human birth story is coupled to Christ's in Luke's Gospel. John's birth is important to Christ's Advent. And amazingly, our advent story is important to Christ and His Advent. We were set apart from the foundation of time to enter into Christ's redeeming work. Our story ties into the cosmic Christ's in a way that is as significant as John's. Though our parents may not have had a visitation from angels, the Holy Spirit entered us at baptism. We were set apart for a holy work, same as John. And even if our parents forgot the details of our birth, God can recount it and one day He will say, "Let me tell you about your birth and about how your life entered, and enters, into My plan for eternity."

THE BIDDING PRAYER

Come, Lord Jesus! (silence)
Ready my spirit to receive You this day. (silence)
Show me how You are at work that I might serve You better. (silence)
Enliven my spirit as I reveal myself to You in written word. (silence)

Then there appeared to him an angel of the Lord, standing at the right side of the altar of incense. When Zechariah saw him, he was terrified; and fear overwhelmed him. But the angel said to him, "Do not be afraid, Zechariah, for your prayer has been heard. Your wife Elizabeth will bear you a son, and you will name him John."

Luke 1:11-13, *NRSV*

THE GOSPEL READING
Luke 1:1-25, *NRSV*

THE REFLECTION
FEAR NOT

While trying to learn Latin two years ago, I was listening in the car to an audio pronunciation guide. One phrase set my ears tingling and became a cheer, chant, and breath prayer. *Nolite timere* (nōLEEtay tĭmĔray) "Fear not." I repeated it over and over again, enough so that my two-and-a-half-year-old son was chorusing with me. It's a phrase scattered throughout the New Testament in a variety of forms. The angel says, "Do not be afraid," in the visitation to Zechariah. *Nolite timere.* Fear not. Mary is soothed with the same words. Jesus grows up and uses the words to settle His disciples' hearts. The phrase marks essential work in God's economy.

Christ wants our fears eased; He wants to calm our waters as He did the raging sea.

Fear is a tempestuous force sometimes at the center of our lives and never farther than the margins. It disrupts our spiritual life and focuses our attention on some event so that we see no good present or coming. God sees this disruption and speaks: "Do not be afraid"— *Nolite timere*. Ours is a time in which fears race across the globe. In a nation with better health and greater wealth, security and freedom than any that has come before, we still quake. We build health and military complexes. We live in gated communities. We stockpile— buying milk, generators and snow-blowers. We are compulsive about making sure someone, or something, doesn't get us.

The Advent message breaks into our fearful lives—our frantic activities—and quiets us. Like Zechariah, we must forcibly be made mute by the Spirit of God—all the voices of distraction falling to the side. He catches us unaware and we are silent enough to hear: "Of his kingdom there will be no end!" *Nolite timere!*

And for you, prey-for-fear beloved of God: "None of this fazes us because Jesus loves us. I'm absolutely convinced that nothing— nothing living or dead, angelic or demonic, today or tomorrow, high or low, thinkable or unthinkable—absolutely *nothing* can get between us and God's love because of the way that Jesus our Master has embraced us" (Romans 8:37-39, *THE MESSAGE*).

NOLITE TIMERE!

THE BIDDING PRAYER

Come, Lord Jesus! (silence)
Ready my spirit to receive You this day. (silence)
Show me how You are at work that I might serve You better. (silence)
Enliven my spirit as I reveal myself to You in written word. (silence)

THE JOURNAL

*In the sixth month the angel Gabriel was sent by God to a town in
Galilee called Nazareth, to a virgin engaged to a man whose name was
Joseph, of the house of David. The virgin's name was Mary. And he
came to her and said, "Greetings, favored one! The Lord is with you."*

Luke 1:26-28, *NRSV*

THE GOSPEL READING
Luke 1:26-38, *NRSV*

THE REFLECTION
ONE FAVORED

How often have we heard in political conversations: "That's in favor
now." We use "favor" in much the same way as "vogue." It marks
something that is passing, just like the changing hairstyles and
faces on the cover of *Vogue* magazine. We want to hitch *our* star to
fashions and people in style, even knowing that fashions change,
people age. Time to find a new ride! It's the American way: Live in
the now, but watch the wind!

Luke uses the word "favor" differently; he uses it in a way that
is full of eternity and God-time. We might think that such a godly
greeting, in which words are put to holy use, would flow gently into
our imaginations and vocabulary. It doesn't. Mary hears the mes-

sage, "Hail, O favored one, the Lord is with you!" and fears it. Mary, like all of us, is not ready to hear a word from the Lord. Humans live with language that is corrupted. We employ words harshly. We hear humanity speaking to us in degraded slang. God-speak has turned to babble. Evil is upon our lips and ears more than we know. But then a word from God breaks in upon us and thoroughly shakes us. These words need illuminating; God-speak must be explained before disbelief turns to recognition. Then the wax falls from our ears. God-language—our mother-tongue—is revived in us, and we say, "Let it be to me according to your word."

A message has broken in on the world and slowly we train our ears to listen for its language; we train our mouths to speak in its syllables. "God has a surprise for you" is the Angel's word, as we read it in *THE MESSAGE*. God is coming into Mary's life, will grow inside her. She will be pregnant with God. This Advent message is for us as well. Before leaving this world, Christ told us, "I am in my Father, and you in me, and I in you" (John 14:20, *NRSV*). We are pregnant with God. God's surprise is ours as well. "Hail O favored one!" Here is favor that lasts.

THE BIDDING PRAYER

Come, Lord Jesus! (silence)
Ready my spirit to receive You this day. (silence)
Show me how You are at work that I might serve You better. (silence)
Enliven my spirit as I reveal myself to You in written word. (silence)

THE JOURNAL

*In those days Mary set out and went with haste to a Judean town
in the hill country, where she entered the house of Zechariah
and greeted Elizabeth. When Elizabeth heard Mary's greeting,
the child leaped in her womb.*

Luke 1:39-41, *NRSV*

THE GOSPEL READING
Luke 1:39-56, *NRSV*

THE REFLECTION
JOY JUMPING

When was the last time you leaped for joy? I can remember leaping
the six feet from the doorway of our bedroom to the bed in order
to do a little jig for my wife, who was just waking from a nap. I had
good news—I'd just been accepted to graduate school. She and I
still refer to the event, reveling in its spontaneity. I see this type of
spontaneity on a daily basis in my three-year-old daughter and
four-year-old son. They're unashamed to skip around the house
in their cartoon underwear, shouting made up words of joy:
"Shahlum, Sháh-áh-lum, Shahlum, Sháh-áh-lum." They are Scrooge
on Christmas Day, the Cubs in the World Series, Mary and Martha
at the empty tomb.

Children are tuned in to such God-rhythms of joy; they're fine-tuned for celebration. It's no miracle that wee little John the baptizer, standing in prenatal waters, did a jig when he heard the Advent news. There was an infusion of Spirit in that room. Everyone was up to their hair follicles in God-presence. The Christ, the Lord, was on the scene and these three human beings were in on His Advent. The scene makes us want to joy-jump still, some 2,000 years later.

Advent causes us to become children again. It is a celebration of birth, a celebration of all that the Christ child shows us about being human. We remember the words of Scripture: "no one can see the kingdom of God without being born from above" (John 3:3, *NRSV*) and "unless you change and become like children, you will never enter the kingdom of heaven" (Matthew 18:3, *NRSV*). Advent calls us back to childhood, back to birth, back to the womb. When we find ourselves as God's children, reborn into a Kingdom of hope, we find our legs again, and find ourselves joy-jumping.

THE BIDDING PRAYER

Come, Lord Jesus! (silence)
Ready my spirit to receive You this day. (silence)
Show me how You are at work that I might serve You better. (silence)
Enliven my spirit as I reveal myself to You in written word. (silence)

THE JOURNAL

Immediately [Zechariah's] mouth was opened and his tongue freed, and he began to speak, praising God.

Luke 1:64, *NRSV*

THE GOSPEL READING
Luke 1:57-80, *NRSV*

THE REFLECTION
A PRAISE UNCORKED

I can remember a few separate occasions when I listened to a story being butchered. I wanted the storyteller to be quiet so that I could put things straight. Though it would have shown better manners to wait my turn, on a few occasions I barged into the conversation to restore the tale. I can also remember a few times when the "inadequate" storyteller barged right back into my tale to set me right. It's hard, almost impossible, to keep our mouths shut about a good story. Zechariah was in on a good story, was perhaps the only person with firsthand knowledge of it, but he had Gorilla Glue on his vocal chords. He was corked up tighter than a Presbyterian church during the Super Bowl.

It's hard for a man not to speak at important gatherings. Circumcision was important for Zechariah. His boy would be named—his name providing *the* significant mark for his life. And here he was, an educated man whose job as priest was to offer prayers and sacrifice for his people—to use his voice for Israel—all bottled up. Nine-plus months of it he'd had. A man with much to say and no way to say it. A word-bomb waiting to explode.

Luke's Advent story readies us to hear something from this man. We hear the story of Mary and Elizabeth sandwiched in the middle of Zechariah's story. Then we get the "lead-in" story that *the woman* is going to name the boy. Nobody in Elizabeth's male-dominated day could believe it. They want Zechariah to say something, even if it has to be written on a tablet. Their looks all said, "C'mon Zechariah, speak up and BE A MAN!" "Do your job here, boy." Zechariah does, but he must do it God's way—emptied of himself.

In silence he writes a message that supports his wife, that backs up her God-spoken naming. Then something remarkable happens. For nine months he's been chewing on God, listening to God-speak attentively, being emptied of male pretension and doubt. His ears have been tuned; his lips have been readying themselves the entire time. What will he say? It can't be another word of disbelief, can it? That's what got him in trouble from the start.

No! Zechariah is a sharp Spirit-instrument. He's primed for this moment. He breaks forth into God-praise. Prophesy comes forth: about the future, about his people, about his son, about a coming savior. Light has dawned and Zechariah, now the only person prepared to speak well, speaks an illuminating word. Like Joseph, Zechariah is emptied of self and refilled so that God has a choice bottle of Advent praise to uncork for the world.

THE BIDDING PRAYER

Come, Lord Jesus! (silence)
Ready my spirit to receive You this day. (silence)
Show me how You are at work that I might serve You better. (silence)
Enliven my spirit as I reveal myself to You in written word. (silence)

THE JOURNAL

In those days a decree went out from Emperor Augustus that all the
world should be registered. This was the first registration . . .

Luke 2:1-2, *NRSV*

THE GOSPEL READING
Luke 2:1-21, *NRSV*

THE REFLECTION
A HEAVENLY LIST

"Census time!" An emperor's order sends an entire world on the move—everyone to their hometown. It turns our minds to all those times the government has asked us to do something, all those times our parents hauled us to school in August to check our name against a roster. We don't like the disruption that comes from needing to jump through bureaucratic hoops, but we also don't want to be left out of something important. We suck it up and obey.

Caesar Augustus is a man who wants people to obey. He's trying to control lives, tax wages, draft men, elicit worship. "Can you believe the chutzpah?" Joseph and Mary must pick up and move for this ruler. Seeing them, we would think these newlyweds are under another's power, like everyone else. Luke's Advent story provides a different light in which to see these sojourners—it is the light of

God's providence. Mary carries within her womb the Lord, the blessed fruit, a baby who is promised "the throne of his father David" and an unending Kingdom. Here is one whose name cannot be commanded by Caesar. He is a new person unable for now to be entered on any roll—He is as yet not officially, not governmentally, named. Yet we've already been allowed to hear the name stored up for Him. The world scene hosts one as yet unnamed, whose name is unlike any on Caesar's list.

It is significant that this Christ, even as He arrives in our world, has His own roll—His own account of persons. His is a list written from the "foundation of the world" (Revelation 13:8, *NRSV*), affected by no earthly ruler. Salvation—not control—is the hallmark of His roster. We are on His list. Christ enters the world controlling world events, in control of where He will be born, who He will serve, what He will do; and in His mind is the knowledge of His holy list. He has come to take an accounting (His own census) of the entire world, to set the world on the move. He is ordering us to our hometown, to His home: "Census time! Your name is written by Me in heaven—written before you were conceived in the womb. Find your name on My roster. And while you're there, look at all the others!"

THE BIDDING PRAYER

Come, Lord Jesus! (silence)
Ready my spirit to receive You this day. (silence)
Show me how You are at work that I might serve You better. (silence)
Enliven my spirit as I reveal myself to You in written word. (silence)

THE JOURNAL

*Now there was a man in Jerusalem whose name was Simeon . . .
It had been revealed to him by the Holy Spirit that he would
not see death before he had seen the Lord's Messiah.*

*There was also a prophet, Anna the daughter of Phanuel . . .
she came, and began to praise God and to speak about the child
to all who were looking for the redemption of Jerusalem.*

Luke 2:25-26,36,38, *NRSV*

THE GOSPEL READING
Luke 2:22-40, *NRSV*

THE REFLECTION
SALVATION WATCHED FOR

Salvation and redemption are not always easy to see. We'd like
them to be happy events, like a cozy birth story. However, nothing
we've read about Jesus' entrance into the world has been cozy.
Salvation and redemption are acts of battle and confrontation, not
things we go looking for without necessity. Luke shows us people
who long for salvation, whose eyes are on the lookout, and he wants
us to develop similar eyes. His Advent story draws us into what
Eugene Peterson has termed "salvation watching."

Simeon and Anna, of all the people, recognize this baby for who He is: the Savior. Why were they able to see Him? What did they have that everyone around them didn't? It's not that they had some special equipment, but that their senses were trained for this salvation watching.

And here is where we see how this cosmic battle is different from any other. Simeon is no *Gladiator*; Anna is no *Xena*. Their training has been God's training, their tools for war His tools: (1) faithfulness to a sacrificial life; (2) a "prayerful expectancy of help for Israel" (Luke 2:25, *THE MESSAGE*); (3) constant worship and fasting; and (4) prayer night and day. Here are warriors so different that they need a new name: *servant*.

Though these servants are allowed to see the salvation of Israel in their old age, they still have no cozy words. This babe, they know, is destined for confrontation. Mark's Advent account has shown us the advent of the battle. Simeon has seen this already: "this child is set for the fall and rising of many in Israel." The battle is already joined; captives are being sought and freed. But the baby's own mother will be pierced through the soul—even she will not be spared from salvation work. He wants to sharpen all those who will recognize Him, hone them "that thoughts out of many hearts may be revealed" as being for Christ, as being salvation watchers.

And "to all who [are] looking for the redemption of Jerusalem"—the redemption of humankind—fellow salvation watchers say, "Did you see that?" "There it is!" "No, no . . . over there!" "Quick, use my binocs!" "You've got to see this up close."

THE BIDDING PRAYER

Come, Lord Jesus! (silence)
Ready my spirit to receive You this day. (silence)
Show me how You are at work that I might serve You better. (silence)
Enliven my spirit as I reveal myself to You in written word. (silence)

THE JOURNAL

PART FOUR

THE FOURTH WEEK OF ADVENT

SEVEN DEVOTIONS FROM JOHN

The Word became flesh and blood, and moved into the neighborhood.

John 1:14, *THE MESSAGE*

THE GOSPEL READING
John 1:1-14, *THE MESSAGE*

THE REFLECTION
AN UPSIDE-DOWN WORD

It's not easy to think of God *becoming* something. We usually think of God as beyond the fray, unaffected by everyday affairs. Becoming entails change—requires being affected by something. The Advent of Christ changes our view of God. We have Christ, the Word, entering our universe, our time and space, and growing from fetus to adulthood. His body is subject to all the limitations and pains to which ours are; He bleeds, sweats, tires, hungers, thirsts and desires. God became fully human, came to involve Himself in our limitation, came to experience lack. Heaven dipped itself down and experienced the consequences that humanity reaped when we lost ourselves to sin.

God's greatest gift to us was to experience what we experience, to know the separation that comes as a consequence of sin. God in the person of Christ became less in order to give us the power to become more. This is part of what my wife has called "our upside-down faith," in which less is more and more is less. As most of us walk into a Christmas full of things and full of providential care, John shows us a model for life. Christ, the King of glory, lowering Himself and walking with His sisters and brothers in their broken condition.

There is hope in this Advent model. The experience of limitation does not diminish Christ. Rather, it provides Him with just what He needs to help us in our infirmity. "For because he himself has suffered and been tempted, he is able to help those who are tempted" (Hebrews 2:18, *RSV*). And for us this Advent season? We are called to become like this Christ, to walk with our brothers and sisters in their brokenness, to dip ourselves down and get dirty that we might lead others to the light— "The true light, which enlightens everyone" (John 1:9, *NRSV*).

THE BIDDING PRAYER

Come, Lord Jesus! (silence)
Ready my spirit to receive You this day. (silence)
Show me how You are at work that I might serve You better. (silence)
Enliven my spirit as I reveal myself to You in written word. (silence)

THE GOSPEL READING*

In the beginning was the Word, and the Word was with God,
and the Word was God. He was in the beginning with God.
All things came into being through him, and without him
not one thing came into being.

John 1:1-3, *NRSV*

THE REFLECTION
CREATIVE WORD

John lets us in on foundational Advent—the "first arrival" we might say. This Advent is described in the first three verses of John's Gospel—lines that are as poetic and beautiful as any recorded. They are a concise creation story describing the source of our world. It's a foundational account speaking to a foundational question oft repeated: "Where did I come from?" John gives us an answer both philosophical and theological.

Archê, the beginning. We've heard this word before in Mark's Gospel story. It rings true in our ears. John has carefully chosen it for his opening. We're at attention, ready to be given an answer to our primordial question. John doesn't miss a beat. The Word, *Logos,* stands at the end of all our questions. We are given an ancestor, a birthright, not some nebulous causal principle or archetypal cosmic fate. We have *Logos*. Personal. Capable of being incarnated. All other questions about the beginning quiet down as we hear about this Being. God's Word, Christ Jesus, is in *archê*, *wording* all things into existence. We are now at the source: original Advent.

As we celebrate Christmas and the Word's incarnation, John reminds us that Christ has been around all along. It's not as if He was uninvolved and then hears about us, only to arrive late. He's been in on the story since moment-one, working His purposes even in a world that has made itself hostile to His voice. The Word speaks through the clanging noise of the fall of humanity and makes itself understood again. Incarnation clears our ears, provides the makings of belief. Belief throws us back to our divine ancestry: "Yes, this is where I came from. This is home."

THE BIDDING PRAYER

Come, Lord Jesus! (silence)
Ready my spirit to receive You this day. (silence)
Show me how You are at work that I might serve You better. (silence)
Enliven my spirit as I reveal myself to You in written word. (silence)

THE JOURNAL

THE GOSPEL READING*

. . . in him was life, and the life was the light of all people. The light shines in the darkness, and the darkness did not overcome it.

John 1:4-5, *NRSV*

THE REFLECTION
BEING LIGHT

106

It's Christmastime and the lights are on; decorations are ablaze across America (to the agitation of amateur astronomers). We're a nation in love with illumination. I've been driving around with my family this week, looking at lights and ornaments, from tasteful to gaudy, from "How did they do that?" to "Why did they do that?" Often I'll hear from the backseat, "Is that *real*, Dad?" Having a philosopher for a father, my children are learning early about "reality," "being" and "existence." Kids reach for reality, want it, do not like it when they're deceived into thinking something is real only to find that it isn't.

We're all reality seekers, or as philosophers like to say, "We're all interested in *being*." John wants to point us to *The Real* and provides a picture in sharp black-and-white images. Like a huge Ansel

Adams photograph, we see the contrasts. The eye is drawn from shadow to light.

Being establishes a world. *The Real* founds life. Christ illuminates existence, our existence, through His own person. The Christ, the light of women and men, bursts into the darkness of a fallen world. And most important for our ears, we are told the darkness has no power over the light.

The image is one of overtaking, like a culprit chasing us down to steal something from us. The darkness wants to chase down the light. But it cannot. Like the words we uttered when we were children, "Can't catch me! Too slow!" the light bursts through the darkness with no fear of being extinguished. It's in hyperdrive. We've found something real in a world of shadows.

I have a few friends who worry about loved ones who've slipped away from the faith. We pray together for these sons, daughters, aunts and fathers who don't listen for Being anymore. It's hard to know what to say. I worry with them. But I pray with the knowledge that God's salvation plan is broader than my own feelings or sight. The light, Christ, enters our lives when we are baptized, when we receive Him. Once there, He is a hard occupant to evict. Darkness fails to overtake Him. I believe this is true for my brothers and sisters who are not listening anymore to the Word made flesh. Ultimately it is Christ's work that saves us, and He has entered a world to take us back—to rescue us. He will leave none of His sisters, none of His brothers behind. His list is prepared. The darkness cannot overtake this work.

THE BIDDING PRAYER

Come, Lord Jesus! (silence)
Ready my spirit to receive You this day. (silence)
Show me how You are at work that I might serve You better. (silence)
Enliven my spirit as I reveal myself to You in written word. (silence)

THE JOURNAL

THE GOSPEL READING*

There was a man sent from God, whose name was John. He came as a witness to testify to the light, so that all might believe through him. He himself was not the light, but he came to testify to the light. The true light, which enlightens everyone, was coming into the world.

John 1:6-9, *NRSV*

THE REFLECTION
HOLY ROAD SIGNS

It's hard not to stand up for yourself in our world, not to want your share of glory and praise. We like to have our works recognized and like it best if we are in a class all to ourselves. Martin Luther King Jr. referred to this as the "Drum Major Instinct." *Who's going to lead the band? I hope it's me.*

This instinct starts early in us; you might even say we're hard-wired for it. (Or perhaps more accurately: We've been rewired for it.) My children love to be first in line, first walking to the car, first to receive their drink, first . . . You name it, they want to be first. Well, except for the bathtub!

John lets us in on another way of living—the God-directed manner of conducting ourselves. He shows us John the baptizer (the first human being entering into His Advent story) providing humanity with a model. Here is what we're supposed to be about. We are to be large road signs for the Christ. Our lives are meant to point everything to Him: praise, blessing, exaltation, even other human beings. All that is good that flows our way is ultimately supposed to be rerouted to Christ. It requires acts of self-death. We must, in a fashion, die.

It's winter as I write these words. I can look out the window and see that life has flowed out of creation, not to be renewed for many months. Trees are bare, bulbs are waiting, blueberry bushes are stick figures against a white Christmas world. Darkness is at its full extent in the Northern Hemisphere. Springtime is distant—something not yet on the anticipation radar. But in these verses from John, we find that spring is not far off—in fact, it is near to us. "The true light that enlightens everyone" has entered a dark winter-world. Spring is Christ, winter our lives. Spring comes as we empty ourselves of the needs to be first. Dying to self, we become barren stick figures with outstretched arms: "There's the Christ! Do you see where my branches point? Spring is that way! Sap flows there. Passions revive in Him."

THE BIDDING PRAYER

Come, Lord Jesus! (silence)
Ready my spirit to receive You this day. (silence)
Show me how You are at work that I might serve You better. (silence)
Enliven my spirit as I reveal myself to You in written word. (silence)

THE JOURNAL

THE GOSPEL READING*

The true light, which enlightens everyone, was coming into the world. He was in the world, and the world came into being through him; yet the world did not know him. He came to what was his own, and his own people did not accept him.

John 1:9-11, *NRSV*

THE REFLECTION
AN UNKNOWN WORD

I'm listening to my kids as they watch a French-English singing video. The tape alternates between French and English verses of songs. They're trying, now and then, to sing in French as they watch, but the songs move fast and they find it hard to keep up. They're out of their element, out of their native tongue.

This is how we come to God. We can't keep up with the language. We've been speaking another tongue for most of human history, babbling absurdities after having lost our native language. So it shouldn't be surprising that when Christ entered the world—a world *He* had made—"the world knew him not." He was the Word we could not understand. We had, for ages, little training in such God-speak.

It's best to have a native speaker help us learn (or relearn) a tongue. Christ became our bilingual guide. He grew from fetus to adulthood with our language—gaining a full grasp of fallen human-speak—and is able to translate God-speak for us in symbol, in parable, in action. The Word become flesh is our sign that translation is available. Immersed in our language, God knows how to offer help, knows how to reacquaint us with His voice.

We are gifted this Christmas with a new language. God-speak has made its Advent in our lives that we might open our ears to this different voice. It is quite significant that belief—belief in His name—comes through hearing. Hearing requires us to be open to new sounds, to new language. Each time we hear, there is a new experience. Recognition is always new; it requires that something strike us newly. Only old sounds fall on deaf ears, like traffic noise we grow used to. Some of the newness lies with us, with our attentiveness, while some of the newness lies in the sound. Christ's message is a sound always new, always *archê*. But we can aid this sound by keeping ourselves primed for God-speak—by studying its meter, cadence and form. Listen freshly to the sounds of *archê*. Hear and believe. Believe and bust out in God-speak—your native tongue.

THE BIDDING PRAYER

Come, Lord Jesus! (silence)
Ready my spirit to receive You this day. (silence)
Show me how You are at work that I might serve You better. (silence)
Enliven my spirit as I reveal myself to You in written word. (silence)

THE JOURNAL

THE GOSPEL READING*

*But to all who received him, who believed in his name,
he gave power to become children of God, who were born, not of blood
or of the will of the flesh or of the will of man, but of God.*

John 1:12-13, *NRSV*

THE REFLECTION
A NAME TO BELIEVE

118

We all want to find someone we can believe in, someone with a
good name. The desire drives our search for heroes and keeps us
attentive to the lives of celebrities. People with good names are not
always easy to find. Investigative reporters continue to narrow our
choices in their daily columns. Scandals are a dime a dozen, with
some of the brightest names belonging to drug or alcohol addicts,
sexual or marital basket cases, or greedy hogs. We've been deadened
to these reports, all too often accepting such lifestyles as inevitable.
Cynicism and fatalism are now the standard reactions.

John puts us back on the right trail. He reorients our searches,
aims our eyes at a worthy mark. "So, you've been looking for something to brighten your lives?" John asks. "You want something to
look up to?" He's been preparing us for these verses, telling us about

the true Light, the true Life, the true Word. All this naming, all the introductory words of explanation concerning the Christ have prepared us for something. "Believe in *this* name!" "Become a child of God!"

Far from discouraging us from searching for heroes, John forces hero worship upon us. We're made for this, but we've got to know who our object is—who won't be in any tabloids today, tomorrow—not ever. Who is worthy of worship? John has already put us in the know. And he says, "Now *receive* Him, *believe* in His name, and *become* His sisters and brothers."

As we believe in this name and worship His person, we are welcomed into a holy family. Such family ties lead us to imitate Christ's model. Our birth is like His holy birth. We are "born, not of blood or of the will of the flesh or of the will of man, but of God." *THE MESSAGE* puts it this way: We're "the God-begotten, not blood-begotten, not flesh-begotten, not sex-begotten" (John 1:12-13). As we've seen, this Christ emptied Himself and was born in the form of a servant. This Advent, may true hero-worship inspire us to be like our holy brother, the only being with a name to believe in.

119

THE BIDDING PRAYER

Come, Lord Jesus! (silence)
Ready my spirit to receive You this day. (silence)
Show me how You are at work that I might serve You better. (silence)
Enliven my spirit as I reveal myself to You in written word. (silence)

THE JOURNAL

THE GOSPEL READING*

And the Word became flesh and lived among us, and we have seen his glory, the glory as of a father's only son, full of grace and truth.

John 1:14, *NRSV*

THE REFLECTION
LIGHT IN A MUCKY WORLD

We're almost there. It's Christmas eve! We've walked through a season of greeting neighbors with "Merry Christmas," of sharing the season in our communities, of worshiping in our churches. We've been involved in acts of community and neighborliness: giving gifts, making cookies, singing carols and decorating our homes for the enjoyment of others. All this has reminded us of the joy and necessity of living in community. God created us for relationship, reflecting the very being of the Trinity.

We don't forget for long, however, that relationship is difficult in our darkened world. We live in a mucky place: full of lies, divorce, anger, abuse and pride. We've all had our share of getting beaten up by living in relationship, and we've all done our share of not respecting those around us. Even on Christmas day there will be hard looks, sore feelings, disappointment and more mixed in with joy and celebration. The healthiest of us keep this to a minimum, while many of us continue to fail miserably at living with other people.

We need to hear John's words this day: "The Word became flesh and lived among us . . . full of grace and truth." Christ enters into the muck to live with us, to be in relation with us. He's the only thing we can see that is *full of grace*. He's bursting with God-speak, bursting with generosity, never tired of our whining, never beating us up. He's light for living with our families, grace for sticking at it with neighbors, balm for our relational hurts.

The Light has come into the world. He asks us to be light to our world, to our neighbors, to all those with whom we come in contact. "In the same way, let your light shine before others, so that they may see your good works and give glory to your Father in heaven" (Matthew 5:16, *NRSV*).

As we spend time opening presents and watching the lights tomorrow, let us remember that we, in whom Christ now dwells, are God's gifts to a dying world. May we be illuminated more and more by Christ, so that we may become good friends and neighbors—persons with whom others long to be in relationship.

THE BIDDING PRAYER

Come, Lord Jesus! (silence)
Ready my spirit to receive You this day. (silence)
Show me how You are at work that I might serve You better. (silence)
Enliven my spirit as I reveal myself to You in written word. (silence)

THE JOURNAL

THE GOSPEL READING
Revisit Your Favorite Gospel Account of Jesus' Advent

THE REFLECTION
TWO ARRIVALS

Christmas Day! For weeks we've been on the lookout for this Christ child, trying to catch glimpses of His grace. We've wanted to be like Mary, pregnant with this person, full up with God. No matter how we've gotten here, whether we've stumbled along in halfhearted reflection or hiked purposefully with eager steps, Christ awaits us in His fullness. It's time to celebrate!

It's just been a couple of years since my wife ran a marathon. My job was to travel in turn to different locations along the course and have provisions ready as she ran by—drinks, sports gels, lotion, Chapstick, ibuprofen. It was thrilling to watch her running toward each pit stop, looking for me. My final stop was the finish line. I can remember waiting there, hoping to see her come down the last gentle hill and through the balloon archway. I people-watched as I waited. There were runners limping across and runners racing to beat their goal time. There were people happy, people grimacing, people looking defeated. Their disposition didn't much matter to the people on the sidelines. Every finisher was greeted with enthusiasm—cheering arose for complete strangers. The more defeated or grumpy a runner looked, the louder the encouragement. It was a grand scene.

Today you've crossed a finish line. You've been running for 20-plus days to see someone—to break through the finish line tape. Look there! Christ is ready to meet you, no matter your disposition. I haven't said much about it until now, but there've been two Advent paths being traveled in your home. Christ's and yours. Christ has been coming—He's been "adventing" again, entering into your heart anew. But you've also been on the move, looking for God, reading devotions as you could, anticipating God-work. As you now come across the goal line, the *how* doesn't matter as much as the *that—that* you've arrived. Like the wise men and shepherds, you've come to see the King. You have arrived at Christmas with Christ and He's cheering for you: "Receive Me. I've a blanket and drink for you . . . some lotion and a massage for your tired feet."

What a joy to know that we have a race partner concerned with us, concerned with the accomplishment, no matter how messy it is! He's the Author of our race and our finish line. In Christ, find yourself renewed today. Pause to drink His refreshment. Take time to rest in Him.

THE BIDDING PRAYER

Come, Lord Jesus! (silence)
Ready my spirit to receive You this day. (silence)
Show me how You are at work that I might serve You better. (silence)
Enliven my spirit as I reveal myself to You in written word. (silence)

THE JOURNAL

ADVENT AND THE NEW CHURCH YEAR

Now that Advent and Christmas have passed, we continue our journey through the Church's calendar year. Advent marks the start of the Church year. After Christmas, we have some weeks until Lent begins. Easter will follow the six weeks of Lent, with Pentecost 50 days after Easter. Following Pentecost, there are the long weeks of Ordinary Time, through summer and fall. Our next Advent seems, right now, to be a long way off. It *is*, from our perspective. We're used to viewing our lives in human time.

Luckily for us, we've sharpened our eyesight and tuned our hearing during the past four weeks. We keep before us the insight from Advent: that eternity broke into our world some two millennia ago. God's salvation story is complete, His list accomplished, His life all that ever can be. It is our ability to participate in eternity, in this God-time, through our imaginative processes, that keeps us from being literally stuck in our day-to-day existence. Each moment that we are blessed to experience is infused with eternity by God, infused with meaning, for He has written all of our stories into His story. Christ, who came to dwell among us, is this mystery of eternity melding with humanity, with temporality. This rings true like the words of the hymn "Christus Paradox" by Sylvia Dunstan: "You the everlasting instant: You, who are our death and our life."[3]

Advent and Christmas are not over for God. Eternity is full of Advent—pregnant with Christ's arrival. Let this be a comfort to us should our hearts sink low in these post-Christmas days.

ADVENT CANDLE-LIGHTING MEDITATIONS FOR CHURCH & HOME

THE FIRST WEEK OF ADVENT
The Gospel of Matthew

Theme: God's Hope

Scripture Readings:

Old Testament: Isaiah 7:10-16
New Testament: Matthew 1:18-25

To Be Read by a Child or Adult Reader: *"Why do we light the first candle?"*

Candle-Lighting Reading:

Emmanuel! . . . God With Us!—Words that stand hopes at attention. We're all ears, asking: "Can it be true?" "A limitless, timeless, all-powerful God bursting into the world to live with *us*?" We want to find truth here. We long to be up-close and personal with such a God. But our hearts, heavy with life-struggles, keep us from hoping too much.

So it is right that we read these Scriptures again today, that we massage our war-beaten hearts with words reminding us of God's gift. A baby, conceived through the power of the Holy Spirit. A child, fully God and fully human. God enfleshed and walking around as our friend. Hope renews at the sound of this Baby-Savior's names: Jesus! Emmanuel! God With Us!

And for our part, we light this first candle to tell everyone about God's hope. Ordinary light. Photons rushing into a darkened world that remind everyone about the true light that has entered the darkness. Jesus. Light of the World. God-enfleshed. Hope-for-tomorrow!

133

Prayer:

God of hope, burst through the darkness this Advent season. Renew Your friendship with us and rekindle our hope for the future.

THE SECOND WEEK OF ADVENT
The Gospel of Mark

Theme: *God's Peace*

Scripture Readings:

> **Old Testament:** Isaiah 40:1-11
> **New Testament:** Mark 1:1-4 and 14-15

To Be Read by a Child or Adult Reader: *"Why do we light the second candle?"*

Candle-Lighting Reading:

We hear voices crying all the time. They go something like this: "Buy this, it'll make you young!"—"Don't you know? You can be somebody!"—"Strike it rich; just use our plan!" They seem to be bringing us good news—gospel—but before long, we find that these voices leave *us* crying . . . literally.

Today's Scripture is an introduction to real gospel, tried-and-true good news. Nobody's trying to sell us anything; nobody's hawking an easy plan. In fact, the message we're given is not directed to our needs at all; instead, it's directed spot-on at the person of God. Isaiah's and Mark's crying is about serving this Lord, getting things ready for His appearance. Attentions get focused on Him and off ourselves. Here is good-news-proper—expansive and spacious. It's full of peace. The kind of peace that comes after a good long cry. The kind of cry that sets you straight.

And for our part, we light this second candle to tell everyone about God's peace-granting gospel. Good news has come, and we get in on it through repentance and belief.

Prayer:

God of peace, we've heard Your cry in our wilderness-lives and we're running back to You, repenting . . . believing. Make us straight, so we can cry Your peace-song in this crooked world.

THE THIRD WEEK OF ADVENT
The Gospel of Luke

Theme: *God's Joy*

Scripture Readings:

Old Testament: 2 Samuel 7:8-17
New Testament: Luke 1:26-38

To Be Read by a Child or Adult Reader: *"Why do we light the third candle?"*

Candle-Lighting Reading:

There's a swirling vortex in our world, a joy-draining vacuum with its nozzle pointing dead-on at our hearts. Fear is its on-switch. Depression and gloom the only things it leaves behind. We see it sucking the life out of our world and we want to turn it off. But our fingers can't reach the switch, the power-cord is welded in, and its siphoning rush is beyond our strength.

David knows the sound of its machinery. Mary has heard its roar. A king whose legacy is not under his control. A virgin whose future isn't under her power. How could they ever have joy? *They've* no power against evil's technology.

Then a voice bursts into their world and ours, saying, "Do not be afraid!" and "Your house and your kingdom will be made sure forever." The voice of God. A voice that fuses their lives to Jesus'! This Jesus stills the rushing vortex . . . silences evil; for it has no power over him.

And what about us? We light this third candle to tell everyone about God's joy. We've been fused to Jesus and we're no longer afraid. For His joyous strength is now ours.

Prayer:

God of joy, we're dancing with David and Mary at the sound of Your voice. Our stories have been united with Christ's and we want to share His joy with a fearful world. Show us how, we pray.

THE FOURTH WEEK OF ADVENT
The Gospel of John

Theme: *God's Love*

Scripture Readings:

    Old Testament: Genesis 2:4-9,15-25
    New Testament: John 1:9-14

To Be Read by a Child or Adult Reader: *"Why do we light the fourth candle?"*

Candle-Lighting Reading:

We've got a gazillion devices to get rid of it: vacuum cleaners, lint rollers, carpet steamers, power washers. We even have special buildings to drive our cars through when they're covered with it. We're talking about "dirt." That four-letter word Mom told us God didn't want any part of. Clean equals "next to godliness." Dirty equals?? *Well . . .* certainly something less godly!

Today's Old Testament Scripture reminds us of an odd little biblical fact. God got His hands dirty and shaped humanity out of the mud. We know from experience that it's back to dirt when we die—*ashes to ashes*, and all that stuff.

But Genesis focuses our attention on an amazing act of love. God didn't just shape little dirtbags. God performed mouth-to-nostril-suscitation, breathing His spirit into the lifeless mud! Divine generosity! God-breathed life!

Alas, we know the history. This life-gift wasn't enough for humanity. We wanted to wallow in the mud, wanted to become less than we were created to be. We fell back to being dirtbags, plain and simple. So our generous God sent another love-gift in the form of a human being. Jesus, full-up with God's Spirit, came to show us that earthen vessels could be full of God. Jesus came to breathe life into us again. Spiritual re-suscitation!

So, today as we await Christmas Day, we light the fourth candle to remind ourselves of our dirty beginning. But more than this! We remind ourselves of God's love-gift of breathed life. Twice given!

Prayer:

God of love, who showers us with life and breath, use these frail earthen vessels for Jesus-work. Fill us through Jesus with the life-breathing Spirit, that we might exhale Your love into this dying world!

AN ADVENT LITANY FOR SMALL GROUPS

I. **Unison Opening Prayer:**

ALL:
Lord, silence in us all voices but Your own,
That in hearing we might believe,
And in believing we might obey,
To the glory of Your name.

II. **The Benedictus (Zachariah's Song; Luke 1:68-79,**
THE MESSAGE):

LEADER:
Let us pray together using the words of Zachariah.

ALL:
Blessed be the Lord, the God of Israel;
  he came and set his people free.
He set the power of salvation in the center of our lives,
  and in the very house of David his servant,
Just as he promised long ago
  through the preaching of his holy prophets:
Deliverance from our enemies
  and every hateful hand;

Mercy to our fathers,
  as he remembers to do what he said he'd do,
What he swore to our father Abraham—
  a clean rescue from the enemy camp,
So we can worship him without a care in the world,
  made holy before him as long as we live.
And you, my child, "Prophet of the Highest,"
  will go ahead of the Master to prepare his ways,
Present the offer of salvation to his people,
  the forgiveness of their sins.
Through the heartfelt mercies of our God,
  God's Sunrise will break in upon us,
Shining on those in the darkness,
  those sitting in the shadow of death,
Then showing us the way, one foot at a time,
  down the path of peace.

III. **Discussion of the Week's Readings**

IV. **The Magnificat (Mary's Song; Luke 1:46-55, *THE MESSAGE*):**

LEADER:
Let us pray together using the words of Mary the mother
  of Jesus.

ALL:
I'm bursting with God-news;
  I'm dancing the song of my Savior God.

God took one good look at me and look what happened—
I'm the most fortunate woman on earth!
What God has done for me will never be forgotten,
the God whose very name is holy, set apart from all others.
His mercy flows in wave after wave
on those who are in awe before him.
He bared his arm and showed his strength,
scattered the bluffing braggarts.
He knocked tyrants off their high horses,
pulled victims out of the mud.
The starving poor sat down to a banquet;
the callous rich were left out in the cold.
He embraced his chosen child, Israel;
he remembered and piled on the mercies, piled them high.
It's exactly what he promised,
beginning with Abraham and right up to now.

V. Silence (5-plus minutes)

VI. Benediction (The Angels' Song; Luke 2:14, *THE MESSAGE*):
ALL:
Glory to God in the heavenly heights,
Peace to all men and women on earth who please him.

VII. Announcements and Prayer Requests

Assignments:

Pray the Magnificat

Read the Christmas Stories:

 The First Week: Matthew

 The Second Week: Mark

 The Third Week: Luke

 The Fourth Week: John

ENDNOTES

1. Abraham Joshua Heschel, quoted in Samuel H. Dresner, ed., *I Asked for Wonder: A Spiritual Anthology / Abraham Joshua Heschel* (New York: The Crossroad Publishing Company, 1995), p. 57.

2. John Donne, "Batter My Heart," *The Harper Anthology of Poetry*, ed. John Frederick Nims (New York: Harper & Row Publishers, 1981), p. 104.

3. Sylvia Dunstan, "Christus Paradox" (Chicago: GIA Publications, Inc., 1991), #G-5463.